CHARLES LETTS · Letts · FOUNDED 1796

LEARNING WITH LETTS

For five- to six-year-olds

Making Friends

Story by Irene Yates
Activities by David Bell, Geoff Leyland, Mick Seller and Irene Yates

Illustrations by Madeleine Baker

People who live in Cherry Walk

For Paul

It was Sunday afternoon in Cherry Walk.

The rain poured down.
It beat on the window panes.
It bounced off the pavements.
It trickled through the gardens.

On a rainy day, sit somewhere you can watch the street outside.

What do people wear?
How do they move?
What happens to plants and trees?
Look closely.
Where are the birds and other animals?

Where does all the rain go?
Find four empty yoghurt pots.
Put them outside in different places to collect water.
Put a stone in each one to stop them from blowing away.

Bring in your pots after one hour.
Which have the most water in? Why?

Mark was bored.
The family had just moved house and he didn't have any friends to play with.

'Why don't you play nicely with your sister?' Mum said crossly.

'Yuk!' said Mark,
but under his breath so no one should hear.

What can you see in the picture?
What's happening at Mark and Kerry's house?

What games do you play when it's raining?

What might have made Mum cross with Mark?
What are Kerry and Mark looking at?

Look out of your windows when it's raining.
What can you see?

Think of different ways to describe rain:
'pouring down'
'lashing down'
'raining cats and dogs'
Draw a picture of it raining 'cats and dogs'
– with real cats and dogs!

Somebody else was feeling very sorry for himself too. Would the rain ever stop? Would the children ever come out to play?

Where is the dog in the picture?
Why is he hiding?
What might he be waiting for?

What else can you see in the playground?
What are they called?
What do they do?

Do you ever go to a playground like this? What do you go on? Which is your favourite: the swings, the slides or . . .? Is there anything you don't like to go on? Why?

'A drop of rain won't hurt us,' Dad grinned.
'Let's put on our macs and wellies
and go for a walk.'

'Count me out,' said Mum.

Guess how many wellies there are.
Count them. Was your guess right?

Guess how many coats are hanging on the pegs. Count them. Was your guess right?

Do you think there would be more coats on the pegs during the summer or the winter?

Guess how many wellies there might be in your home. Now go and count them. Was your guess right? Draw a picture of all your family's wellies.

Mark saw some children eating their Sunday lunch.

'Do you think they'll come out to play when they've finished?' he asked Dad.

What can you see in the picture?
Why does Mark want the children to come out when they've finished their lunch?

Who's waiting for Mark in the playground? Does Mark know?
What might happen?

Make up a story about the little girl at the window. Who is she?
What does she want to do?
You could draw some pictures to go with your story.

Splish! Splosh! Splash!
went Mark in the puddles.

Kerry noticed a playground sign.
Mark began to cheer up a bit.
'Can we go in, Dad? Can we?'

Find a nice big puddle with a dry area around it, or make your own puddle.

Put your wellies on and stand in the puddle. Take six steps out of the puddle on to dry ground. What have you left behind?

How many footprints can you make before your wellies become dry? Try riding through your puddle on a bike or scooter. Look at the tracks left behind. How long do they take to dry up?

What happens to your puddle when the sun comes out?

'Let's have a look in the paper shop window,' Dad said.

'I bet they're all going to the playground,' said Mark. 'Come on, come on!'

What kind of shop is this?
What does it sell?

What is Dad doing?
What might they be reading about?
What do the notices say?

Are there cards like these in your local shop windows? Next time you go to the shop, look for cards with the same words as the ones in the picture.

Imagine you have lost a pet or a favourite toy. Make a card and draw a picture of your lost toy or pet to go in your local shop window.

Dad and Kerry sauntered along.
How Mark wished they would hurry up!

Everyone else had arrived at the playground before them.

How many children can you find in the picture? How many grown-ups can you see?

All the children and grown-ups in the picture are in small groups.
Each group has the same number of people in it.
Count how many are in each group.
How many groups are there?

‘I knew we’d be last!’ Mark said.
‘Now there’s nothing left to go on.’

‘Rubbish!’ laughed Dad. ‘Off you go.’

‘But we don’t know anybody,’ Kerry said shyly.

What's happening in the picture?
The little girl is jumping on ________ .
A boy is sliding down ________ .
A girl is climbing up ________ .
A dog is sitting under ________ .

Why don't Mark and Kerry rush to play?
How do you think Kerry feels?
Do you ever feel shy?
What makes you shy?

What could Kerry and Mark do
to make friends?

'Higher! Higher! Higher!'
chuckled the girl on the swing.

Can you find things on which you go up high?
Point to the child
who is the highest.

Can you find things on which you go fast? Which of the children in the playground do you think is going the fastest?

What things in the playground are made of wood?
What things are made of metal?
Are there some which might be both metal and wood?

A boy came over to Kerry and Mark.
He looked exactly like the boy who was pushing the swing.

'My name's Wesley,' he said smiling.
'That's Charley. We're twins.
And that's Rose on the swing.
Coming to play?'

Why do Charley and Wesley look exactly alike? Do you know any twins? Are they exactly alike? How do you know Kerry and Mark aren't twins?

Do you look like someone else in your family?

Tell someone who hasn't read this story – your Mum or Dad – about one of the children in the picture. Say what they look like, but don't say whether they are a boy or a girl. Can your Mum or Dad find the child?

Kerry and Mark forgot all about being shy and rushed off to the slide with Wesley.

Find a tray or lid with a smooth surface. Find some books to put under one end to make a slide.

Slide some of your favourite toys down it. Which slides the best? Why do you think this is?

Try making the slide higher with more books. Try making the slide lower with less books. Which makes the toys go faster?

‘There’s Jenny from next door with her Mum.
And that’s their baby,’ said Kerry.

Talk about who you can see on the roundabout. Why is Jenny holding on so tightly? How can you tell if the baby is enjoying himself?

Why is Mum on the roundabout with the baby? Why isn't it safe to sit the baby on it on his own?

Why is the dog happy now?

What might happen next?

The rain clouds drifted away and
the sun came out.
Chat, chat, chat went the mums and dads.

Off came everybody's coats.
On went Kerry and Mark's trainers.

Collect pairs of shoes and wellies from all around your home and put them together in a large jumble.

Put all the shoes into pairs.
Sort them according to who wears them.
Make a pile of shoes for a dry day, and a pile for a rainy day.

The shoe pile can be sorted in many other ways.
Muddle all the shoes up again.
How many other ways can you think of to sort them?

It was Sunday afternoon in Cherry Walk.

The sun was shining like mad.
And everybody was friends!

Talk about what the children are doing in the picture. Point to each child. What is her or his name? Where is the dog?

Whose Mum can you see? Whose Dad can you see?

Make up a story of your own, called 'Friends'. Ask someone to help you make the story into a little book. Draw pictures to show what happens. Write some words to help tell the story.

If you need ideas, read this story again and look at the pictures.

Activity notes

Pages 2–3 This activity is all about careful observation: 'look closely' are the key words. Let your child suggest reasons why some pots have more water in than others.

Pages 4–5 These kinds of questions take children beyond the story, encouraging them to think things out and draw on their own experiences. There are many phrases in the English language which sound very silly (especially to children) when interpreted literally. Talking about such phrases together will help your child acquire greater understanding of language.

Pages 6–7 Deciding 'where', 'what' and 'why' about the dog involves using clues, both from the picture and earlier in the story. Relating the story to your child's own experience will help to bring it alive. You could take the questions a stage further, eg 'How do you make a swing work?' 'What does a roundabout do?'

Pages 8–9 Developing the ability to guess or estimate sensibly is an important practical mathematical skill. Although it is hard to teach, children will become more proficient the more they can practise this skill.

Pages 10–11 Children have an instinctive understanding of what makes a good story when it is read to them. When your child is making up stories, you could ask questions like, 'What is the little girl like? Is she friendly?' Paying attention to details in this way will help story-writing skills at a later stage.

Pages 12–13 This activity introduces the idea of evaporation. Encourage your child to think about where the water has gone as the tracks and puddles dry up.

Pages 14–15 Reading notices, postcards and signs will help your child understand that writing carries meaning and messages. Learning to read real-life or 'environmental' print is now seen as an important part of developing reading skills. Writing postcards together and sending them to friends or family is an enjoyable way for children to practise early writing skills.

Pages 16–17 Simple multiplication begins when children group objects together and then add up the number of groups. It is always better to begin with groups of two, three or four, as these are numbers that young children can handle with ease.

Pages 18–19 Using a character in a story who might feel shy or sad, helps children to identify feelings and to talk more easily about their own feelings. At a later stage, this should help them to make their story writing more true to life.

Pages 20–21 This activity encourages children to use comparing words. It also involves sorting, an important skill in maths, as well as science.

Pages 22–23 Asking your child to talk about someone in the picture will help them to describe accurately, and to begin to use more descriptive vocabulary, eg 'This child has long, curly hair'. A variation on this would be to ask them to describe someone you both know.

Pages 24–25 This activity helps your child to see that the steeper the angle of the slide, the faster the toys go down.

Pages 26–27 Part of enjoying reading is thinking about what's happening in the pictures as well as the story, and relating it to what you already know. Children enjoy being able to tell you how characters are thinking and feeling, and making sensible guesses about why things are happening. Making inferences in this way is an important step forward.

Pages 28–29 A simple sorting activity which helps to develop classifying skills. Other ways in which shoes can be sorted are heavy/light, bendy/stiff, by colour, etc.

Pages 30–31 Helping your child to make a little book will give them a sense of achievement and ensure that writing becomes a pleasurable experience, not a chore. Typing out the story – on a word processor or a typewriter – will enhance the appearance of your child's work and give them a real sense of pride.

About the authors and advisers

Irene Yates is a writer and teacher in charge of language development at Lakey Lane School in Birmingham.

David Bell is Assistant Director of Education (Forward Planning) for Newcastle upon Tyne City Council, a former primary head and maths specialist.

Geoff Leyland is Deputy Head of Deer Park Primary School in Derbyshire and a former science and technology advisory teacher.

Mick Seller is Deputy Head of Asterdale Primary School in Derbyshire and a former science and technology advisory teacher.
Elizabeth Bassant is a language advisory teacher in Haringey, London. **Peter Ovens** is Principal Lecturer for Curriculum and Professional Development at Nottingham Polytechnic and a science specialist. **Peter Patilla** is a maths consultant, author and Senior Lecturer in Mathematics Education at Sheffield Polytechnic.
Margaret Williams is an advisory teacher for maths in Newton Abbott, Devon.